Congressional Research Service

Noncitizen Eligibility for Federal Public Assistance: Policy Overview and Trends

Ruth Ellen Wasem
Specialist in Immigration Policy

September 27, 2012

Congressional Research Service

7-5700

www.crs.gov

RL33809

CRS Report for Congress ————————

Prepared for Members and Committees of Congress

Summary

The extent to which residents of the United States who are not U.S. citizens should be eligible for federally funded public aid has been a contentious issue for more than a decade. This issue meets at the intersection of two major policy areas: immigration policy and welfare policy. The eligibility of noncitizens for public assistance programs is based on a complex set of rules that are determined largely by the type of noncitizen in question and the nature of services being offered. Over the past 16 years, Congress has enacted significant changes in U.S. immigration policy and welfare policy. Congress has exercised oversight of revisions made by the 1996 welfare reform law (the Personal Responsibility and Work Opportunity Reconciliation Act, P.L. 104-193)—including the rules governing noncitizen eligibility for public assistance that it established—and legislation covering programs with major restrictions on noncitizens' eligibility (e.g., food stamps/SNAP, Medicaid).

This report deals with the four major federal means-tested benefit programs: the Supplemental Nutrition Assistance Program (SNAP, formerly food stamps), the Supplemental Security Income (SSI) program, Temporary Assistance for Needy Families (TANF) block grant programs, and Medicaid. Laws in place for the past 15 years restrict the eligibility of legal permanent residents (LPRs), refugees, asylees, and other noncitizens for most means-tested public aid. Noncitizens' eligibility for major federal means-tested benefits largely depends on their *immigration status*; whether they arrived (or were on a program's rolls) before *August 22, 1996*, the enactment date of P.L. 104-193; and how long they have lived and worked in the United States.

LPRs with a substantial work history or military connection are eligible for the full range of programs, as are asylees, refugees, and other humanitarian cases (for at least five to seven years after entry). Other LPRs must meet additional eligibility requirements. For SNAP, they generally must have been legally resident for five years or be under age 18. Under TANF and SSI, they generally are ineligible for five years after entry and then eligible at state option. States have the option of providing Medicaid to pregnant LPRs and children within the five-year bar. Unauthorized aliens (often referred to as illegal aliens) are not eligible for most federal benefits, regardless of whether they are means tested, with notable exceptions for emergency services, (e.g., Medicaid emergency medical care or Federal Emergency Management Agency disaster services).

TANF, SSI, food stamp, and Medicaid recipiency among noncitizens decreased over the 1995-2005 period, but has inched upwards in 2011. While the 10-year decrease was affected by the statutory changes, the poverty rate of noncitizens had also diminished over the 1995-2005 decade. The poverty rate for noncitizens residing in the United States fell from 27.8% in 1995 to 20.4% in 2005. It has risen to 24.3% in 2011. Noncitizens are disproportionately poorer than native-born residents of the United States.

This report does not track legislation and is updated as policy changes warrant.

Contents

Figures

Tables

Appendixes

Contacts

Introduction

The extent to which residents of the United States who are not U.S. citizens should be eligible for federally funded public aid has been a contentious issue since the 1990s. This issue meets at the intersection of two major policy areas: immigration policy and welfare policy. Over the past 16 years, Congress has enacted significant changes in U.S. immigration policy and welfare policy. Congress has exercised oversight of revisions made by the 1996 welfare reform law (the Personal Responsibility and Work Opportunity Reconciliation Act, P.L. 104-193)—including the rules governing noncitizen eligibility for public assistance that it established—and legislation covering programs with major restrictions on noncitizens' eligibility (e.g., food stamps/SNAP, Medicaid).

This report deals with the four major federal means-tested benefit programs: the Supplemental Nutrition Assistance Program (SNAP, formerly food stamps), the Supplemental Security Income (SSI) program, Temporary Assistance for Needy Families (TANF) block grant programs, and Medicaid. It is organized into four main parts: an overview of existing eligibility law for the four programs and the policies that preceded the 1996 act; an overview of related immigrant policies affecting eligibility (specifically, the treatment of sponsored aliens); an analysis of trends in noncitizen poverty and benefit use; and a summary of the eligibility rules for aliens residing in the United States illegally. Appendices at the conclusion elaborate on the specifics of current eligibility rules for the four major programs.

Overview of Alien Eligibility Law

Pre-1996 Program Policies

Prior to the major amendments made in 1996, there was no uniform rule governing which categories of noncitizens were eligible for which government-provided benefits and services, and there was no single statute where the rules were described. Alien eligibility requirements, if any, were set forth in the laws and regulations governing the individual federal assistance programs.

Summarizing briefly, lawful permanent residents (i.e., immigrants) and other noncitizens who were legally present (e.g., refugees) were generally eligible for federal benefits on the same basis as citizens in programs where rules were established by law or regulation. These included major public assistance programs like Aid to Families with Dependent Children (AFDC, the predecessor of TANF), the SSI program, food stamps, and Medicaid. With the single exception of emergency Medicaid, unauthorized (illegally present) aliens were barred from participation in all the major federal assistance programs that had statutory provisions for noncitizens, as were aliens legally present in a temporary status (i.e., nonimmigrants such as persons admitted for tourism, education, or employment).

However, many health, education, nutrition, income support, and social service programs did not include specific provisions regarding alien eligibility, and unauthorized aliens were potential participants.[1] These programs included, for example, the Special Supplemental Nutrition Program

---

[1] For discussion of these issues, see CRS Report RL34500, *Unauthorized Aliens' Access to Federal Benefits: Policy and Issues*, by Ruth Ellen Wasem.

for Women, Infants, and Children (the WIC program), child nutrition programs, initiatives funded through the Elementary and Secondary Education Act, the Earned Income Tax Credit (EITC), community and migrant health centers, and the Social Services Block Grant (SSBG) program.

The 1996 Welfare Reform Law

Title IV of the Personal Responsibility and Work Opportunity Reconciliation Act of 1996 (PRWORA, P.L. 104-193) established comprehensive new restrictions on the eligibility of noncitizens for means-tested public assistance—with significant exceptions for those with a substantial U.S. work history or military connection. For legal permanent residents (LPRs) who were resident as of enactment of the law (August 22, 1996), the act generally barred eligibility (food stamps and SSI) or allowed it at state option (Medicaid and TANF). For food stamps and SSI benefits, LPRs entering after August 22, 1996, (new entrants) also were denied eligibility, with no time constraint. On the other hand, new entrants applying for Medicaid and the newly established Temporary Assistance for Needy Families (TANF) program were barred for five years after their entry, and then allowed eligibility at state option. Refugees and asylees were *allowed* eligibility for five years after entry/grant of status, then made ineligible (unless they became citizens or qualified under another status). Nonimmigrants (i.e., aliens on temporary visas) and unauthorized aliens were barred from almost all federal programs.

Post-1996 Revisions

The 1996 changes made in the alien eligibility rules proved controversial, particularly the termination of benefits for recipients who were receiving benefits or for legal residents of the United States as of the date the new welfare law was enacted, August 22, 1996.

The SSI termination date for these recipients was extended from August 22, 1996, to September 30, 1997, by P.L. 105-18, signed into law on June 12, 1997. More extensive modifications to the new alienage rules were then included in P.L. 105-33, the 1997 Balanced Budget Act, signed into law on August 5, 1997. It amended the welfare reform law to provide that legal immigrants who were receiving SSI as of August 22, 1996, continue to be eligible, regardless of whether their claim was based on disability or age. Additionally, those who were here by August 22, 1996, and subsequently become disabled were made eligible for SSI.

Food stamp eligibility was expanded by provisions of P.L. 105-185, the Agricultural Research, Extension, and Education Reform Act of 1998. Eligibility was extended to several groups of LPRs who were here as of August 22, 1996: elderly (65+) persons (not including those who become 65 after August 22, 1996); individuals receiving government disability benefits (including those who become disabled after August 22, 1996); and children (persons who were under 18 as of August 22, 1996, until they become adults). Amendments in P.L. 105-33 and P.L. 105-185 extended the period of food stamp/SSI/Medicaid (but not TANF) eligibility for refugees and asylees from five to seven years.

During the 107th Congress, P.L. 107-171, the "farm bill," contained substantial changes to food stamp eligibility rules for noncitizens, expanding food stamp eligibility to include the following groups:

- all LPR children, regardless of date of entry (it also ended requirements to deem sponsors' income and resources to these children);

- LPRs receiving government disability payments, so long as they pass any noncitizen eligibility test established by the disability program (e.g., SSI recipients would have to meet SSI noncitizen requirements in order to get food stamps/SNAP); and

- all individuals who have resided in the United States for five or more years as "qualified aliens"—that is, LPRs, refugees/asylees, and other non-temporary legal residents (such as Cuban/Haitian entrants).[2]

- The changes to rules for the disabled became effective October 1, 2002; new rules for children were effective October 1, 2003; and the five-year residence rule went into effect April 1, 2003.

Subsequent laws have resulted in additional revisions, as follows:

- In 2007, §525 of the Consolidated Appropriations Act for FY2008 (P.L. 110-161) permitted Iraqi and Afghan aliens who had been granted special immigrant status under §101(a)(27) of the INA eligible for resettlement assistance, entitlement programs, and other benefits available to refugees admitted under §207 of the INA for a period not to exceed six months. Also, §409 of the Consolidated Appropriations Act prohibited funds from being used to provide homeowners assistance to foreign nationals who are neither an alien lawfully admitted for permanent residence, nor authorized to be employed in the United States.

- P.L. 110-328 extends to nine years (during FY2009 through FY2011) the period of eligibility of certain refugees, asylees, and aliens in other specified humanitarian categories for SSI benefits, provided that the alien has a pending naturalization application or makes a declaration that he or she has made a good faith effort to pursue U.S. citizenship. It also made victims of trafficking among the eligible population. As a result of this provision, the specified LPR must additionally fit within one of several categories, which include being an LPR for less than six years, applying for LPR status within four years of beginning to receive SSI, being at least age 70, or being under age 18.[3]

- The Children's Health Insurance Program Reauthorization Act of 2009 (CHIPRA 2009, P.L. 111-3) allows states to waive—for children and pregnant women who are LPRs and battered individuals lawfully residing in the United States—key elements of PRWORA: the statutory bar, the limited eligibility provision, and the five-year bar, and thus gives states the option of providing Medicaid and State Children's Health Insurance Program (CHIP) to children and pregnant women who are LPRs and battered individuals (described in section 431(c) of PRWORA) lawfully residing in the United States during the first five years that they are living in the United States.[4]

---

[2] Although the conference agreement did not explicitly adopt the Senate proposal to lift the current seven-year limit on eligibility for refugees and asylees, adoption of a five-year legal residence rule would effectively eliminate it. Also see **Appendix C** "Qualified Aliens."

[3] Those under 18 would not be subject to the naturalization or declaration requirement., as a person must be 18 years old in order to file a naturalization petition.

[4] For a complete analysis, see CRS Report R40144, *State Medicaid and CHIP Coverage of Noncitizens*, by Ruth Ellen Wasem.

Current Eligibility Policy

Under current law, legally resident noncitizens' eligibility for the major federal means-tested benefit programs depends on their immigration status; whether they arrived (or were on a program's rolls) before August 22, 1996 (the enactment date of P.L. 104-193); their work history and military connection; their length of legal residence; and how states have exercised their options to allow program participation by noncitizens.[5] Following significant changes made by the 1997, 1998, and 2002 amendments noted above, the *basic* rules now are as follows:[6]

- Refugees and asylees are eligible for food stamps/SNAP.

- Refugees and asylees are eligible for SSI benefits and Medicaid for seven years after arrival, and are eligible for TANF for five years.[7] After this term, they generally are ineligible for SSI, but may be eligible, at state option, for Medicaid and TANF. As noted above, there is a time-limited extension of SSI for nine years through FY2011 for refugees and asylees waiting to naturalize.

- LPRs with a substantial work history—generally 10 years (40 quarters) of work documented by Social Security or other employment records—or a military connection (active duty military personnel, veterans, and their families) are eligible for the full range of programs.

- LPRs receiving SSI as of August 22, 1996, continue to be eligible for SSI.

- Medicaid coverage is required for all otherwise-qualified SSI recipients (they must meet SSI noncitizen eligibility tests).

- Disabled LPRs who were legal residents as of August 22, 1996, are eligible for SSI.

- Disabled LPRs are eligible for food stamps/SNAP.[8]

- LPRs who were elderly (65+) and legal residents as of August 22, 1996, are eligible for food stamps/SNAP.

- LPRs who have been legal residents for five years or are children (under 18) are eligible for food stamps/SNAP.

- LPRs entering after August 22, 1996, are barred from TANF and Medicaid for five years, after which their coverage becomes a state option.[9] States have the

---

[5] In addition, "deeming" rules (discussed later in this report) may affect eligibility.

[6] **Appendix A** lays out these rules in more detail, including special rules that apply to several limited noncitizen categories: certain "cross-border" American Indians, Hmong/ Highland Laotians, parolees and conditional entrants, and cases of abuse. **Appendix C** presents the basic eligibility rules from a different perspective, using a new term/category—"qualified alien"—established by the 1996 welfare reform law but not otherwise used in immigration or welfare law.

[7] Refugee/asylee treatment is accorded to Cuban/Haitian entrants, certain aliens whose deportation/removal is withheld for humanitarian purposes, Vietnam-born Amerasians fathered by U.S. citizens, and victims of human trafficking. For those aliens who arrive in the United States without one of these forms of humanitarian relief, the seven- or five-year period begins after the date the aliens receive the status.

[8] For SSI eligibility, disabled LPRs must meet SSI permanent and total disability standards. For food stamp eligibility, disabled LPRs must be receiving governmental benefits for disability (e.g., SSI, Social Security disability payments, certain veterans disability benefits).

[9] This five-year ban on eligibility for new entrants also applies to a program closely related to the Medicaid program— (continued...)

option to cover LPRs who are children or who are pregnant during the first five years. For SSI, the five-year bar for new entrants is irrelevant because they generally are denied eligibility (without a time limit).

Citizens of the Freely Associated States

Citizens of the Freely Associated States (FAS, which are the Marshall Islands, Micronesia, and Palau) are afforded certain immigration-related benefits that enable them to travel freely to and from the United States in a legal status akin to nonimmigrants.[10] Citizens of the FAS who come from the Republic of the Marshall Islands (RMI) and the Federated States of Micronesia (FSM) are permitted to live, study, and work in the United States in accordance with the Compact of Free Association Amendments Act of 2003 (Compact, P.L. 108-188).[11] FAS citizens are not considered LPRs under the Immigration and Nationality Act, but they are permitted to acquire LPR status if otherwise eligible.[12] While in the United States, FAS citizens from the RMI and FSM are able to document their legal status with their RMI or FSM passports and the I-94 arrival/departure card issued to them when they enter the United States. FAS citizens from the Republic of Palau do not benefit from the immigration provisions in the Compact that permit those from the RMI or FSM to seek employment, go to school, or establish a residence. Citizens of the Republic of Palau only need to present an appropriate travel document, such as a valid passport or a certified birth certificate, to enter the United States.[13]

Under current law, FAS citizens are not eligible for federal public benefits (except emergency services and programs expressly listed, such as Medicaid emergency medical care or Federal Emergency Management Agency disaster services). Prior to 1996, FAS citizens residing in the United States were able to obtain federal assistance because they were considered "permanently residing under color of law" (PRUCOL), which is an eligibility standard that is not defined in statute. Historically, PRUCOL has been used to provide a benefit to certain foreign nationals who the government knows are present in the United States, but whom it has no plans to deport or remove.[14] When Title IV of P.L. 104-193 established comprehensive limitations and requirements on the eligibility of all noncitizens for means-tested public assistance, it effectively ended access to federal benefits for foreign nationals who had been considered PRUCOL. As a consequence,

---

(...continued)

the State Children's Health Insurance Program (CHIP). It is the only categorical noncitizen eligibility rule affecting CHIP. The U.S. Department of Health and Human Services (HHS), however, promulgated regulations in 2002 allowing states to provide CHIP coverage to fetuses. Since fetuses do not have an immigration status, states arguably can use this option to provide prenatal care services to pregnant women, regardless of their immigration status. *Fed. Reg.* v. 67, pp. 61955–74, October 2, 2002.

[10] Nonimmigrants are foreign nationals admitted to the United States for a temporary period of time and an expressed purpose. For a complete discussion of nonimmigrants, see CRS Report RL31381, *U.S. Immigration Policy on Temporary Admissions*, by Ruth Ellen Wasem.

[11] The Compact of Free Association Act of 1985 (P.L. 99-239) as amended by the Compact of Free Association Amendments Act of 2003 (P.L. 108-188).

[12] For a discussion of the circumstances under which they would be subject to federal taxes, see CRS Report RS21732, *Federal Taxation of Aliens Working in the United States*, by Erika K. Lunder.

[13] For the documentation FAS citizens must have in order to work in the United States, see U.S. Citizenship and Immigration Services (USCIS), Office of Business Liaison, *Employment Bulletin*, v. 106, Dec. 8, 2004.

[14] For further information on PRUCOL, see CRS Report RL34500, *Unauthorized Aliens' Access to Federal Benefits: Policy and Issues*, by Ruth Ellen Wasem.

---

citizens of the FAS residing in the United States are barred from receiving most federal public benefits.

Related Immigrant Policies Affecting Eligibility: Sponsorship and Deeming

"Public Charge"

Historical Development

Opposition to the entry of foreign paupers and aliens "likely at any time to become a public charge"—language found in the Immigration and Nationality Act (INA) today—dates from colonial times. A bar against the admission of "any person unable to take care of himself or herself without becoming a public charge" was included in the act of August 3, 1882, the first general federal immigration law. Over time, a policy developed in which applicants for immigrant status can overcome the public charge ground for exclusion based on their own funds, prearranged or prospective employment, or an *affidavit of support* from someone in the United States.

An affidavit of support on behalf of a prospective immigrant had to be submitted as necessary by one or more residents of the United States in order to provide assurance that the applicant for entry would be supported in this country. Starting in the 1930s and continuing until the 1980s, affidavits of support were administratively required by what was then the Immigration and Naturalization Service (INS) but had no specific basis in statute or regulation. Court decisions beginning in the 1950s generally held that affidavits of support were not legally binding on the U.S. resident sponsors.[15] The unenforceability of affidavits of support led to the adoption of legislation in the late 1970s and early 1980s intended to make them more effective (see the discussion of "deeming" of income and financial resources below).

1996 Immigration Law Reforms

The Illegal Immigration Reform and Immigrant Responsibility Act of 1996 (IIRIRA, Division C of P.L. 104-208), coupled with the 1996 welfare reform law, altered the obligations of persons who sponsor immigrants arriving or adjusting to LPR status in the United States. The IIRIRA standards, which are part of the INA, cover requirements for sponsors, mandatory affidavits for family immigrants, and sponsorship liability, as follows:

- The person petitioning for the immigrant's admission must be the sponsor signing the affidavit of support.

- Sponsors must demonstrate the ability to maintain an annual income of at least 125% of the federal poverty line (100% for sponsors who are on active duty in U.S. Armed Forces), *or* share liability with one or more joint sponsors, each of whom must independently meet the income requirement.

---

[15] *Department of Mental Hygiene v. Renal*, 6 N.Y. 2d 791 (1959); *State v. Binder*, 356 Mich. 73 (1959).

- All family-based immigrants as well as employment-based immigrants who are coming to work for relatives must have affidavits of support filed for them.

- Sponsors who fail to support sponsored aliens are legally liable to the sponsored aliens and to any government agency that provides sponsored aliens needs-based assistance. As modified by the 1996 immigration law, a sponsor's liability ends when the sponsored alien is no longer subject to deeming, either through naturalization or meeting a work test.[16]

- Since passage of IIRIRA, the affidavit of support is a legally binding contract enforceable against the affiant (i.e., sponsors) if the immigrant collects any means-tested benefit.[17] Upon notification that a sponsored alien has received designated means-tested benefits, the federal, state, or local entity which provided the benefit must request the sponsor's reimbursement for an amount equal to the cost of the benefit.[18] If the sponsor fails to respond to the request within 45 days, the agency may commence an action in federal or state court.[19] There is a 10-year limit on actions to obtain reimbursement.[20]

In the context of Medicaid, §214 of CHIPRA 2009 (P.L. 111-3) states: "no debt shall accrue under an affidavit of support against any sponsor of such an alien on the basis of provision of assistance to such category and the cost of such assistance shall not be considered as an unreimbursed cost." According to the legislative language, this provision applies only to LPRs who are covered under §214 of that act; that is, LPRs who are pregnant or children, whom the state opts to provide CHIP and Medicaid during their first five years in the United States.

"Deeming" of Income and Resources

Pre-1996 Policy

In response to concerns about the unenforceability of affidavits of support and the perceived abuse of the welfare system by some newly arrived immigrants, legislation was enacted in the late 1970s and early 1980s limiting the availability of SSI, food stamps/SNAP, and Aid to Families with Dependent Children (AFDC) to sponsored immigrants. The enabling legislation for these programs was amended to provide that—for the purpose of determining financial eligibility—immigrants who had used an affidavit of support to meet the public charge requirement would be deemed to have a portion of their immigration sponsors' income and resources available to them.

---

[16] This work test is similar to the one applied in determining noncitizens' eligibility for public assistance—attaining a substantial work history of 10 years (40 quarters of documented work).

[17] 8 C.F.R. § 213a.1 defines "means-tested public benefit." This includes food stamps/SNAP, Medicaid, Supplemental Security Income (SSI), and Temporary Assistance for Needy Families (TANF).

[18] 8 U.S.C. § 1183a(b)(2). Despite the mandatory nature of the statutory language, Congress may lack constitutional authority to compel states to request reimbursement of state funds from sponsors, and the statute itself recognizes that the states have discretion on whether to follow up requests with further legal action.

[19] 8 U.S.C. § 1183a(b)(2)(A).

[20] 8 U.S.C. § 1183a(b)(2)(C).

Post-1996 Requirements

The 1996 welfare reform law and the Illegal Immigration Reform and Immigrant Responsibility Act of 1996 significantly expanded the use of sponsor-to-alien deeming as a means of restricting the participation of new immigrants in federal means-tested programs.[21] Both deeming and the affidavits of support upon which deeming is based are intended to implement the provision of the INA that excludes aliens who appear "likely at any time to become a public charge."

The new deeming rules (primarily set out in the 1996 welfare reform act) are designed to make it more difficult for sponsored aliens to meet financial tests for benefits—even if they pass the "categorical" eligibility test by being in an eligible class of noncitizen. They apply to aliens who enter after December 19, 1997 (the effective date of the new affidavit of support) and who apply for TANF, Medicaid, SSI, or food stamps/SNAP. Under these rules, *all* of the income and resources of a sponsor (and a sponsor's spouse) may be deemed available to the sponsored applicant for assistance until the noncitizen becomes naturalized or meets a work test. Previous law contained specific deeming requirements only for SSI, food stamps, and AFDC (TANF's predecessor); only a portion of a sponsor's income and resources was deemed to the sponsored applicant; and deeming lasted for three years after entry (with a brief five-year rule for SSI).[22] Since it is §213A of the INA that makes the affidavits of support legally binding, some policy makers use "213A" as shorthand to identify who is covered by the deeming rules.

When IIRIRA made an affidavits of support a legally binding contract as discussed above, it also directed the Attorney General to include "appropriate information" regarding affidavits of support in the Systematic Alien Verification for Entitlements (SAVE) system. While Congress did not specify exactly what information was to be included in the SAVE system, it did require the Attorney General to establish an automated record of the sponsors' social security numbers.[23] The SAVE system enables federal, state, and local governmental agencies to obtain immigration status information to determine eligibility for public benefits. The goal of the system is to aid eligibility workers in determining an applicant's immigration status to ensure that only entitled applicants receive public benefits.[24]

Trends in Noncitizen Poverty and Benefit Use

The eligibility rules for "means-tested" benefits are, by design, linked to income and poverty among other criteria (e.g., citizenship status and family structure). This portion of the report analyzes poverty among the foreign born and follows with a comparative analysis of benefit use

---

[21] Enacted as Division C of the Omnibus Consolidated Appropriations Act for 1997 (P.L. 104-208), signed into law on September 30, 1996.

[22] The deeming period under SSI was five years from January 1994 through September 1996.

[23] "The Attorney General shall ensure that appropriate information regarding the application of [affidavits of support] is provided to the system for alien verification of eligibility (SAVE)" P.L. 104-208, §551(a); See also §213A(i)(2) of INA.

[24] SAVE's statutory authority dates back to the Immigration Reform and Control Act of 1986 (IRCA). IRCA mandated immigrant status verification of applicants for AFDC, Medicaid, unemployment compensation, and food stamps/SNAP, and required an individual who is not a citizen or national of the United States to present documentation of alien status, which shall be used to verify the alien's immigration status with the INS through an automated or other system. IRCA specified that the federal government would reimburse the states and any other entity charged with immigrant status verification 100% of the cost incurred by implementing and operating the status verification system.

for the four major federal means-tested benefit programs: food stamps/SNAP, Supplemental Security Income (SSI), Temporary Assistance for Needy Families (TANF) cash assistance, and Medicaid.

Noncitizen Poverty Levels

One of the most comprehensive sources of information on the foreign born is the U.S. Census Bureau's March Current Population Survey (CPS). The Census Bureau conducts the CPS each month to collect labor force data about the civilian noninstitutionalized population. The March Supplement of the CPS gathers additional data about income, education, household characteristics, and geographic mobility. Because the CPS is a sample of the U.S. population, the results are estimates. Additionally, while the data distinguish between the foreign born who have naturalized and those who have not, they do not distinguish between types of noncitizens (e.g., permanent, temporary, illegal).[25]

General Trends

The number of noncitizens who are poor has remained rather steady despite a substantial increase in the number of foreign born over the past decade, as **Figure 1** illustrates. The total number of foreign born residents of the United States went from an estimated 24.5 million in 1995 to 40.0 million in 2012, and the number of those who were not citizens went from an estimated 16.6 million in 1995 to 22.0 million in 2012. During this same period, the estimated number of noncitizens in poverty, defined as below 100% of the poverty level, dropped slightly from 4.6 million in 1995 to 4.4 million in 2005, then rose to 5.4 million in 2011.[26] More significant to the eligibility for federal assistance programs, the estimated number of naturalized citizens in poverty rose from 0.8 million in 1995 to 2.2 million in 2011. This shift among the foreign-born citizens and noncitizens may be due to a variety of factors, including the aging of the naturalized population (and resulting diminished earnings), increased naturalization rates, and the earning potential of newer, higher-skilled immigrants.

---

[25] The CPS began collecting immigration data on the foreign born in 1994, and the first years were plagued by problems of weighting, particularly with the Asian population in the sample, and by over-reporting of naturalization by the foreign born. Most of these problems appear to have been resolved by 1996.

[26] For an explanation of how poverty levels are calculated, CRS Report RL33069, *Poverty in the United States: 2011*, by Thomas Gabe.

Figure 1. Noncitizen Residents in Poverty, 1994-2011

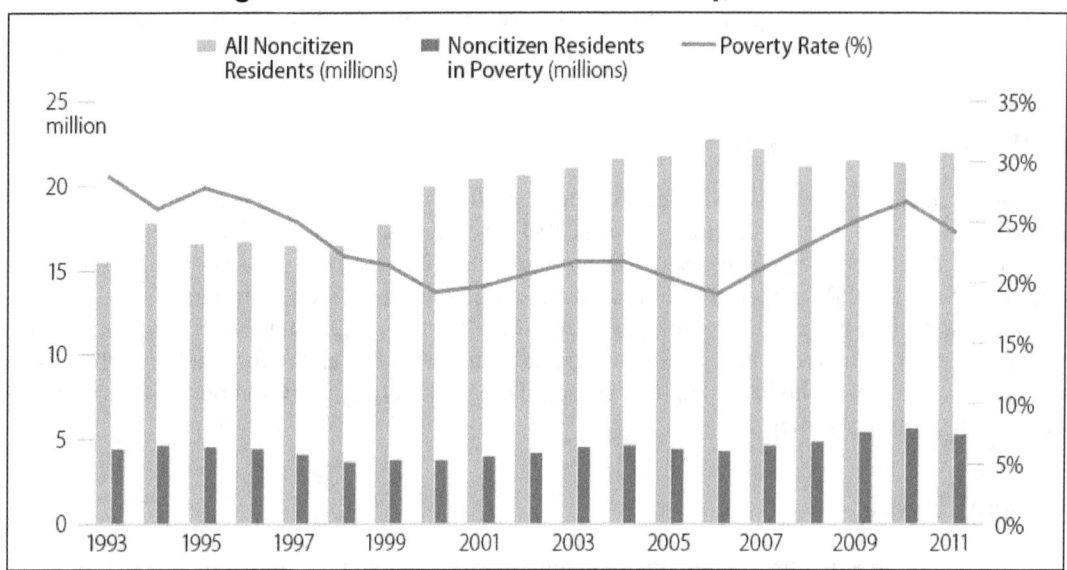

Source: CRS analysis of the CPS March Supplements, 1994-2012.

Table 1. Poverty by Citizenship Status, 1995 and 2011

(estimated in millions)

	1995	2012/2011
Total population	263.733	308.456
Estimated poor	36.425	46.247
Poverty rate	13.8%	15.0%
Naturalized citizens	7.904	17.934
Estimated poor	0.833	2.233
Poverty rate	10.5%	12.5%
Noncitizens	16.623	22.032
Estimated poor	4.619	5.353
Poverty rate	27.8%	24.3%

Source: CRS analysis of CPS by Thomas Gabe. Population totals in the CPS are based on 2012 data and the poverty data in the 2012 CPS are based on 2011 income.

Comparative Analysis

Noncitizens appeared to be disproportionately poorer than native-born residents of the United States, as **Table 1** shows. Noncitizens had an estimated poverty rate of 24.3%, in contrast to a poverty rate of 15.0% for the total population in 2011. Naturalized citizens had the lowest poverty rate of the three groups (12.5%) in 2011. Notably, the poverty rate for noncitizens residing in the United States has fallen from 27.8% in 1995.[27]

Figure 2 provides a more detailed comparison of the change over the past 16 years in poverty by citizenship status by grouping the CPS data into three poverty levels in comparison to the total population: below 100% of poverty, from 100% to 199% of poverty, and at or above 200% of poverty. Despite being an increasing share of the total population, the foreign born (naturalized citizens and noncitizens) have remained a steady portion of those below 100% of poverty. Noncitizens are poorer in comparison to their share of the total population. There are a variety of factors that contribute to this variation, not the least of which are education and skill levels, naturalization rates, and length of residency in the United States.

Figure 2. Comparative Poverty Levels by Citizenship, 1995, 2005, and 2011

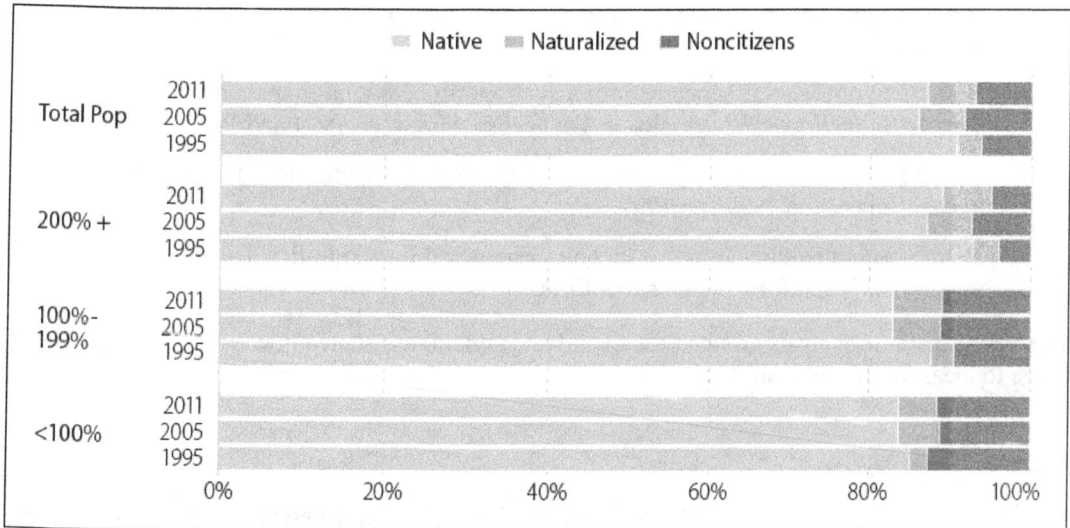

Source: CRS analysis of the CPS March Supplements, 1996, 2006, and 2012.

Noncitizen Benefit Use

Formative Research

In 1995, the Congressional Research Service (CRS) analyzed data from the March 1994 CPS (the first CPS to ask participants about their citizenship status) that indicated that the foreign born were significantly more likely to use SSI, but were not significantly more likely to use AFDC or food stamps.[28] In AFDC, food stamps, and Medicaid, noncitizens had higher participation rates than the native born, but naturalized citizens had lower participation rates than the native born. However, in the SSI program both noncitizens and naturalized citizens had higher participation rates than native-born citizens. This finding was especially true among the aged population.[29]

---

[27] For general statistics on poverty, see CRS Report RL33069, *Poverty in the United States: 2011*, by Thomas Gabe.

[28] The CRS analysis analyzed three categories of citizenship status: native-born citizens, naturalized citizens, and noncitizens, which are based on subchapter III of the INA. 8 U.S.C. §§ 1401-1452 and § 1101(a)(3).

[29] Archived CRS Report 95-276, *Native and Naturalized Citizens and Noncitizens: An Analysis of Poverty Status,* (continued...)

In addition to the elderly, the other major subgroup of the foreign born using welfare appeared to be noncitizens from refugee-sending countries. While the 1995 CRS study did not disaggregate refugees, Urban Institute analysts did try to do so in Senate testimony. Based also on the March 1994 CPS, they found that 13.1% of foreign born from the major refugee sending countries used AFDC, SSI, or general assistance, compared to 5.8% of foreign born from other countries.[30]

The Urban Institute continued to analyze the CPS for noncitizen use of welfare and found changes in usage from 1994 to 1997. Noteworthy among the principal findings of the later Urban Institute study were the following:

- Use of public benefits among noncitizen households fell more sharply than among citizen households between 1994 and 1997, 34% and 14% respectively.

- Those noncitizens imputed to be refugees experienced declines (33%) that were at least as steep as other noncitizens despite the fact that most refugees continued to be eligible for benefits in 1997.

- Noncitizen households accounted for a disproportionately large share of the overall decline in welfare caseloads that occurred between 1994 and 1997.

- Welfare usage among elderly immigrants and naturalized citizens did not appear to change between 1994 and 1997.

- Neither naturalization nor rising incomes accounted for a significant share of noncitizens' exits from public benefit use.

The Urban Institute analysis grouped use of SSI and general assistance in with AFDC/TANF usage to measure overall welfare receipt.[31]

Recent Findings

More recently, CRS analysis of the March 2006 and 2012 CPS indicated public assistance usage was down generally from 1995 to 2005 for all four programs (**Figure 3**). The trend has reverse in 2009 and 2011 for Medicaid and SNAP, and the percentage usage now surpasses 1995 levels. Percentage use of TANF and SSI have gone up slightly in 2011. CPS data are self-reported and generally understate the actual number of program beneficiaries. It is not possible to determine whether the increased focus on immigration's costs and benefits may have suppressed noncitizens' reporting of public assistance.[32] Nonetheless, the downward shifts in usage after enactment of PWORA are consistent with those observed previously and are comparable to the general findings of the Urban Institute and others. The recent increases track the Great Recession and broader trends.

(...continued)

Welfare Benefits, and Other Factors, by Michael O'Grady.

[30] Fix, M., Passel, J.S., & Zimmermann, W. (1996). *The use of SSI and other welfare programs by immigrants.* Testimony before the U.S. Senate [Judiciary] Subcommittee on Immigration, February 6, 1996. Washington, DC: The Urban Institute.

[31] Fix, M., & Passel, J.S., (1999).*Trends in Noncitizens' and Citizens' Use of Public Benefits Following Welfare Reform: 1994-97.* Washington, D.C.: The Urban Institute.

[32] CRS Report R42053, *Fiscal Impacts of the Foreign-Born Population*, by William A. Kandel.

Figure 3. Percentage of Noncitizens Receiving Selected Assistance of Benefits: 1995, 1998, 2005, 2009, and 2011

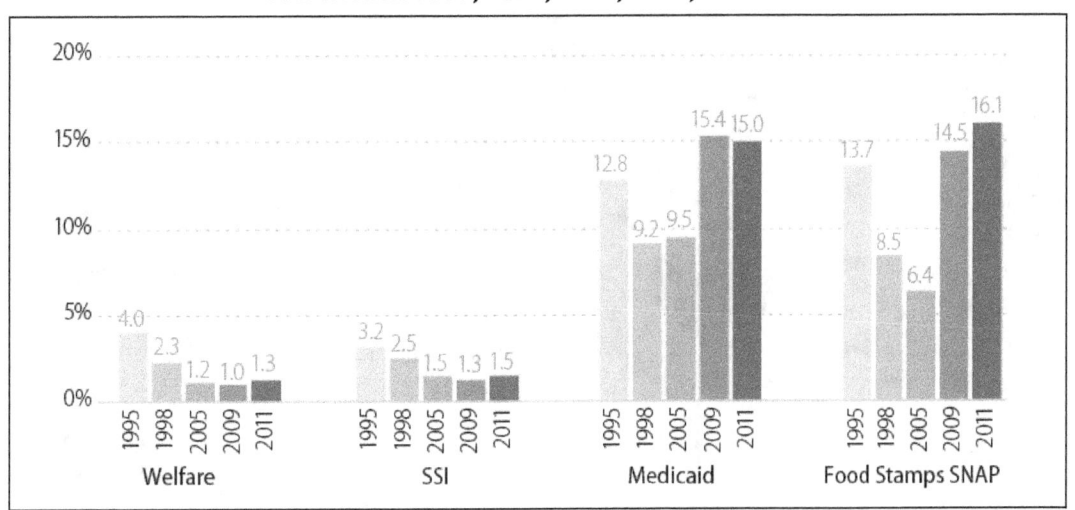

Source: CRS analysis of the CPS March Supplement, 1996, 1999, 2006, 2010, and 2012.

Notes: Food stamp/SNAP data are by households; all other data are individuals. Welfare includes AFDC, TANF and general cash assistance.

What is most intriguing from the latest analysis is that these general declines in program beneficiaries are not evidenced consistently across the programs or among the three citizenship groupings. As in the 1995 CRS study, this CRS analysis focused on three categories of citizenship status: native-born citizens, naturalized citizens, and noncitizens. The benefit use patterns for naturalized persons in the CPS samples offer exceptions to the general trends, as **Figure 4** presents. Benefit receipt decreased in estimated total numbers for noncitizens in TANF, food stamps/SNAP, and SSI, as detailed in **Appendix B**. The estimated participation of naturalized citizens rose in TANF, SSI, food stamps/SNAP, and Medicaid. The substantial increase in immigration throughout the 1990s and into the 2000s is one of many factors that may be affecting these trends, as are general economic and labor force factors and family structures.[33]

As **Figure 4** illustrates, the estimated percentage of the welfare recipients (defined here as individuals who reported receipt of AFDC, TANF, or general cash assistance) who were noncitizens rose slightly from 1995 (11.8%) through 2011 (13.2%), even though the total caseload fell substantially. The estimated proportion of welfare recipients who were naturalized citizens increased from 2.3% in 1995 to 5.0% in 2011.

---

[33] For analysis of immigration trends over this time period, see CRS Report RL32235, *U.S. Immigration Policy on Permanent Admissions*, by Ruth Ellen Wasem.

**Figure 4. Percentage Distribution of Recipients by Citizenship
Status: 1995 and 2011**

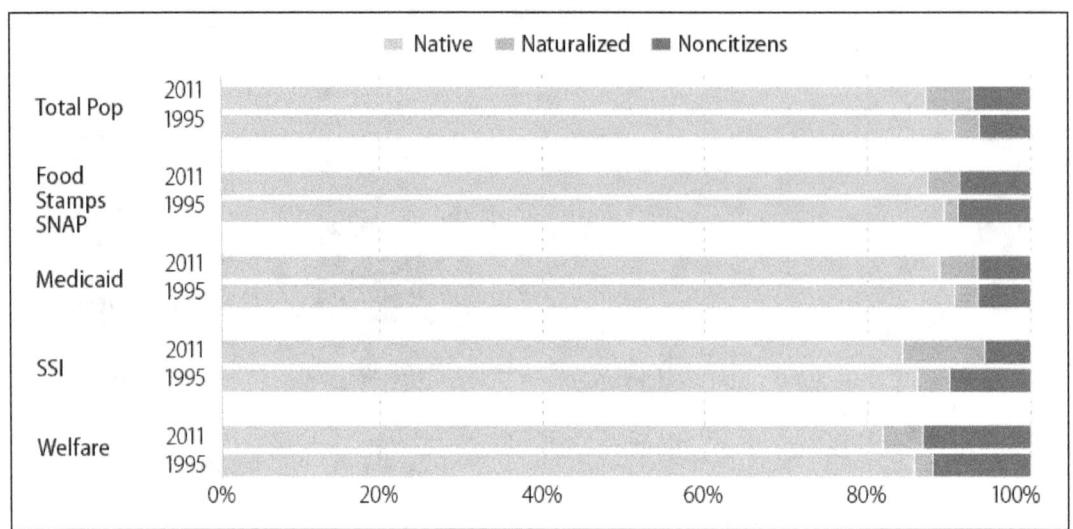

Source: CRS analysis of the CPS March Supplement, 1996 and 2012.

Notes: Food stamp data are by households; all other data are individuals. Welfare includes AFDC, TANF and general cash assistance.

Estimates of SSI usage from the CPS suggest a different pattern, one in which noncitizen usage decreased from 9.9% in 1995 to 5.6% in 2011. Receipt of SSI among the naturalized increased from 3.9% to 10.0% over the 15-year period. (**Figure 4**).

Both naturalized citizens as a percentage of Medicaid recipients rose from 1995 to 2011, 2.9% to 4.6%. Noncitizens as a percent of Medicaid recipients remained at 6.5%. Among natives, however, there was a decline over the decade (**Figure 4**). It is important to note that reporting of Medicaid use in the CPS is reportedly plagued with problems.[34]

CPS estimates of households receiving food stamps/SNAP indicate a similar pattern from 1995 to 2011. Similar to SSI, the proportion of recipients who are naturalized citizens notably increased. The percentage of reported food stamp recipients who were noncitizens in 2011 was 8.8%.

Program Participation Data

Analysis of SSI, TANF, and food stamp program participation data offers another perspective on changes in noncitizen receipt of public assistance over time. (The administrative data for the Medicaid program does not provide time series statistics on citizenship status.) These analyses also reveal the ebb and flow of noncitizen program participation. We cannot assume, however, that the program participation data always record a change in citizen status when a noncitizen beneficiary naturalizes. The most recent data available are for FY2009 for TANF and 2010 for SSI and SNAP.

---

[34] For further discussion, see U.S. House of Representatives Committee on Ways and Means, *2004 Green Book: Background Material and Data on the Programs Within the Jurisdiction of the Committee on Ways and Means*, chapter 15, Medicaid, March 2004.

Figure 5. Noncitizens as a Percentage of all Food Stamp/SNAP, SSI, and TANF/AFDC Cash Assistance, 1989-2010

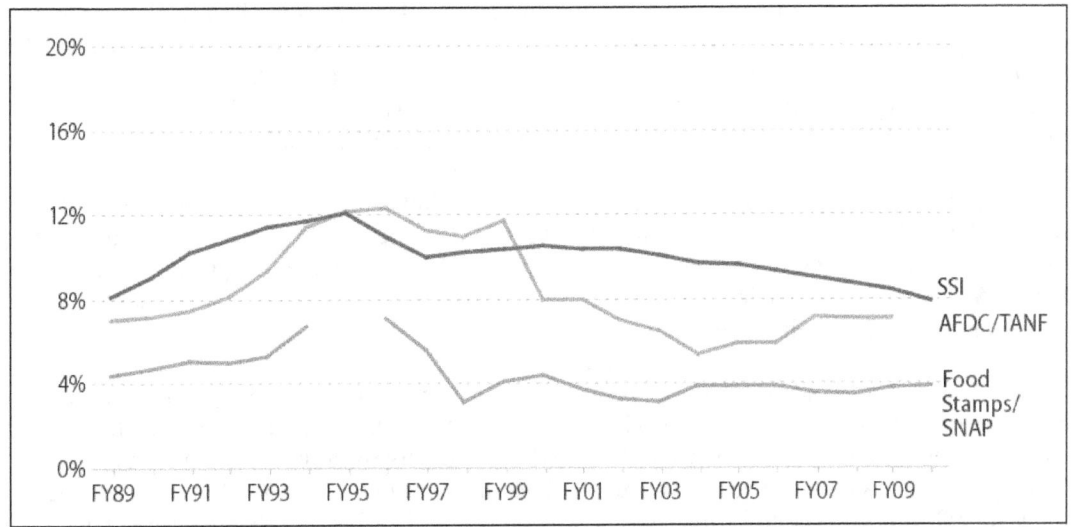

Source: CRS presentation of data published annually by the Social Security Administration, the DHHS Administration for Children and Families, and the USDA Food Stamp Quality Control Samples. Food stamp data are not available for FY1995.

Supplemental Security Income (SSI)

The percentage of the SSI caseload that were noncitizens has dipped slightly in recent years, after inching upward in the 1980s and early 1990s, as **Figure 5** depicts. It stood at 8.7% (or 655,988 participants) in 2009 after peaking at 12.1% (or 785,410 participants) in 1995. In 2008, noncitizens accounted for 26.9% of all aged SSI recipients, down from a high of 31.8% in 1995. Noncitizens accounted for 5.3% of disabled (or blind) recipients in 2008, down from 6.3% in 1995. In 2010, 7.9% of all SSI recipients were noncitizens.[35]

Food Stamps/SNAP

As illustrated in **Figure 5**, food stamp participation by noncitizens rose during the early 1990s, then dropped by the late 1990s. The peak occurred in 1996 when 1.8 million noncitizens comprised 7.1% of the 25.5 million food stamp recipients. The most recent available data from the U.S. Department of Agriculture (USDA) SNAP Quality Control Samples estimated that noncitizens receiving food stamps/SNAP stood at 3.9% in FY2010.[36]

---

[35] CRS Report 94-486, *Supplemental Security Income (SSI)*, by Umar Moulta-Ali.

[36] CRS Report R41374, *Reducing SNAP (Food Stamp) Benefits Provided by the ARRA: P.L. 111-226 and P.L. 111-296*, by Randy Alison Aussenberg, Jim Monke, and Gene Falk; CRS congressional distribution memorandum, *Noncitizen Verification for the Supplemental Nutrition Assistance Program (SNAP)*, by Ruth Ellen Wasem, July 30, 2012 (available upon request).

Cash Assistance

The actual number of families or persons who receive TANF benefits is not known because there is no comprehensive reporting on families receiving the range of TANF benefits and services. The Department of Health and Human Services (HHS), however, does collect data on families receiving ongoing assistance—most frequently cash welfare. The number of families receiving cash welfare peaked in March 1994 at 5.1 million and dropped to 1.6 million in June 2008.[37]

The HHS data on characteristics of these TANF recipients indicate that, as a percentage of total adult TANF cash assistance recipients, noncitizens legally in the United States who receive TANF (formerly AFDC) increased from 7.0% in FY1989 to 12.3% in 1996, then dropped to 7.1 in 2009. **Figure 5** illustrates this curvilinear trend of noncitizen usage. These data exhibit the same trend as that of the TANF recipients generally.

Most states have not exercised their option to bar LPRs from TANF. According to the CRS State Noncitizen Eligibility Survey (SNES), 34 states and Washington, DC, reported in 2002 that they are exercising the option to provide TANF to LPRs after the five-year bar ends. In terms of funding, 27 states and Washington, DC, reported that they used their own funds as well as federal funds in 2000 and 2002 to cover the costs of providing TANF to those LPRs who were in the United States prior to the passage of the 1996 welfare reform act. Twenty-six states and the U.S. Virgin Islands reported that they used their own funds as well as federal funds to cover the costs of providing TANF to those LPRs who were excluded (e.g., barred first five years) or whose eligibility had expired (e.g., refugees after five years).[38] Data from the 2004/2006 SNES for the most part indicate a continuation of these policies.

Federal and State Benefit Eligibility Standards for Unauthorized Aliens

Federal Benefits[39]

Unauthorized aliens (often referred to as illegal aliens) are not eligible for most federal benefits, regardless of whether they are means tested. The class of benefits denied is broad. The scope of the bar on unauthorized aliens hinges on how broadly the clause "federal public benefit" is implemented. The law defines this clause to be

> (A) any grant, contract, loan, professional license, or commercial license provided by an agency of the United States or by appropriated funds of the United States; and (B) any retirement, welfare, health, disability, public or assisted housing, postsecondary education, food assistance, unemployment benefit, or any other similar benefit for which payments or

---

[37] CRS Report RL32760, *The Temporary Assistance for Needy Families (TANF) Block Grant: Responses to Frequently Asked Questions*, by Gene Falk.

[38] CRS Report RL32363, *State Policies on Immigrant Eligibility for Temporary Assistance for Needy Families (TANF)*, by Ruth Ellen Wasem.

[39] For a more complete analysis, see CRS Report RL34500, *Unauthorized Aliens' Access to Federal Benefits: Policy and Issues*, by Ruth Ellen Wasem.

assistance are provided to an individual, household, or family eligibility unit by an agency of the United States or by appropriated funds of the United States.[40]

So defined, this bar covers many programs whose enabling statutes do not individually make citizenship or immigration status a criterion for participation. Thus, unauthorized aliens are statutorily barred from receiving benefits that previously were not individually restricted—Social Services Block Grants, and migrant health centers, for example—unless they fall within the 1996 welfare act's limited exceptions. These statutory exceptions include the following:

- treatment under Medicaid for emergency medical conditions (other than those related to an organ transplant);[41]

- short-term, in-kind emergency disaster relief;

- immunizations against immunizable diseases and testing for and treatment of symptoms of communicable diseases;

- services or assistance (such as soup kitchens, crisis counseling and intervention, and short-term shelters) designated by the Attorney General as: (i) delivering in-kind services at the community level, (ii) providing assistance without individual determinations of each recipient's needs, and (iii) being necessary for the protection of life and safety; and

- to the extent that an alien was receiving assistance on the date of enactment, programs administered by the Secretary of Housing and Urban Development, programs under title V of the Housing Act of 1949, and assistance under Section 306C of the Consolidated Farm and Rural Development Act.[42]

PRWORA sought further to prevent unauthorized aliens from receiving the Earned Income Tax Credit (EITC) by also requiring that the social security numbers (SSN) of recipients (and spouses) be valid for employment in the United States.[43]

P.L. 104-193 also states that individuals who are eligible for free public education benefits under state and local law shall remain eligible to receive school lunch and school breakfast benefits. (The act itself does not address a state's obligation to grant all aliens equal access to education under the Supreme Court's decision in *Plyler* v. *Doe*.) Beyond these nutrition benefits, the act neither prohibits nor requires a state to provide unauthorized aliens other benefits funded under the National School Lunch Act or the Child Nutrition Act, or under the Emergency Food Assistance Act, Section 4 of the Agriculture and Consumer Protection Act, or the Food Distribution Program on Indian Reservations under the Food Stamp Act.

---

[40] §401(c) of PRWORA, 8 U.S.C. 1611.

[41] For analysis, see CRS Report RL31630, *Federal Funding for Unauthorized Aliens' Emergency Medical Expenses*, by Alison Siskin.

[42] Subtitle E of Title V of the Illegal Immigration Reform and Immigrant Responsibility Act (Division C of P.L. 104-208) later facilitated the removal of unauthorized aliens from housing assistance. For analysis, see CRS Report RL31753, *Immigration: Noncitizen Eligibility for Needs-Based Housing Programs*, by Alison Siskin and Maggie McCarty.

[43] CRS Report R42628, *Ability of Unauthorized Aliens to Claim Refundable Tax Credits*, by Erika K. Lunder et al..

State Benefits

Unlike earlier federal law, P.L. 104-193 expressly bars unauthorized aliens from most state and locally funded benefits. The restrictions on these benefits parallel the restrictions on federal benefits. Unauthorized aliens are generally barred from state and local government contracts, licenses, grants, loans, and assistance.[44] The following exceptions are made:

- treatment for emergency conditions (other than those related to an organ transplant);

- short-term, in-kind emergency disaster relief;

- immunization against immunizable diseases and testing for and treatment of symptoms of communicable diseases; and

- services or assistance (such as soup kitchens, crisis counseling and intervention, and short-term shelters) designated by the Attorney General as: (i) delivering in-kind services at the community level, (ii) providing assistance without individual determinations of each recipient's needs, and (iii) being necessary for the protection of life and safety.

Also, the restrictions on state and local benefits do not apply to activities that are funded in part by federal funds; these activities are regulated under the 1996 law as federal benefits. Furthermore, the law states that nothing in it is to be construed as addressing eligibility for basic public education. Finally, the 1996 law allows the states, through enactment of new state laws, to provide unauthorized aliens with state and local benefits that otherwise are restricted.[45]

Despite the federally imposed bar and the state flexibility provided by the 1996 law, states still may be required to expend a significant amount of state funds for unauthorized aliens. Public elementary and secondary education for unauthorized aliens remains compelled by judicial decision, and payment for emergency medical services for unauthorized aliens remains compelled by federal law. Meanwhile, certain other costs attributable to unauthorized aliens, such as criminal justice costs, remain compelled by the continued presence of unauthorized aliens.[46]

[44] For further analysis, see CRS Report RL34345, *State and Local Restrictions on Employing, Renting Property to, or Providing Services for Unauthorized Aliens: Legal Issues and Recent Judicial Developments*, by Kate M. Manuel, Jody Feder, and Alison M. Smith.

[45] For further analysis, see CRS Report RS22500, *Unauthorized Alien Students, Higher Education, and In-State Tuition Rates: A Legal Analysis*, by Jody Feder.

[46] For a fuller discussion, see CRS Report RL33431, *Immigration: Frequently Asked Questions on the State Criminal Alien Assistance Program (SCAAP)*, by Karma Ester.

Appendix A. Noncitizen Eligibility for Selected Major Federal Programs

Class of Alien	Food Stamps/SNAP	SSI	TANF	Medicaid
Legal permanent residents (LPRs):				
—without a substantial (generally 10-year) work history,[a]	Ineligible for 5 years after entry, except:	Ineligible until naturalized, except	Eligibility required for persons with a military connection.	Same as TANF, *plus* coverage required for SSI recipients. (*Note:* Eligible for emergency medical services.)
	(1) persons with a military connection,	(1) persons with a military connection,	Eligibility at state option for persons resident in the U.S. as of August 22, 1996.Post-August 22, 1996, entrants: ineligible for 5 years after entry, then eligible at state option.	Eligibility at state option for pregnant LPRs and children, regardless of the date of entry.
	(2) persons resident in the U.S. as of August 22, 1996, and age 65+ at the time,	(2) persons receiving SSI benefits as of August 22, 1996, and		
	(3) persons receiving disability benefits, and	(3) persons resident in the U.S. as of August 22, 1996, and now disabled (eligible for SSI disability benefits).		
	(4) children under age 18.	(*Note:* Disabled children are included as eligible if resident in the U.S. as of August 22, 1996.)		
—with a substantial (generally 10-year) work history,[a]	Eligible.	Eligible.	Eligible.	Eligible.
Military connection:				
—aliens with a military connection (active duty military personnel, honorably discharged veterans, and their immediate families).	Eligible.[b]	Eligible.[b]	Eligible[b].	Eligible.[b]
Humanitarian cases:				
—asylees, refugees, Cuban/Haitian entrants, Iraqi and Afghan special immigrants, certain aliens whose deportation/removal is being withheld for humanitarian reasons, and Vietnam-born Amerasians fathered by U.S. citizens.[c]	Eligible after entry/grant of such status.	Eligible *for 7 years* after entry/grant of such status. Ineligible after 7 years unless naturalized or if in receipt of SSI benefits as of August 22, 1996.	Eligible *for 5 years* after entry/grant of such status. Eligible at state option after 5 years.	Eligible *for 7 years* after entry/grant of such status. Eligible at state option after 7 years.

Class of Alien	Food Stamps/SNAP	SSI	TANF	Medicaid
Special Cases:				
—noncitizen "cross-border" American Indians,[d]	Eligible.	Eligible.	Eligible at state option.	Eligible.
—Hmong/Highland Laotians,[e]	Eligible.	Eligible only if individual meets eligibility criteria for another noncitizen category—e.g., as a legal permanent resident, asylee, refugee, person with a military connection.	Same as SSI. (*Note:* LPRs eligible above under conditions noted above for TANF treatment of LPRs.)	Same as SSI. (*Note:* LPRs eligible under conditions noted above for Medicaid treatment of LPRs.)
—parolees and conditional entrants,[f]	Eligible.	Eligible only if individual: (1) has a military connection, (2) was receiving SSI as of August 22, 1996, or (3) was resident in the U.S. as of August 22, 1996, and is now disabled (eligible for SSI disability benefits).	Eligible if resident as of August 22, 1996. Ineligible for 5 years after entry, if entry is post-August 22, 1996. Otherwise eligible at state option.	Same as TANF.
—cases of abuse (battery or extreme cruelty).[g]	Eligible.	If not eligible as an LPR or humanitarian case, then eligible if the individual: (1) has a military connection, (2) was receiving SSI as of August 22, 1996, or (3) was resident in the U.S. as of August 22, 1996, and is now disabled (eligible for SSI disability benefits).	Eligible if resident as of August 22, 1996. Ineligible for 5 years after entry, if entry is post-August 22, 1996. Otherwise eligible at state option.	Eligibility at state option
—victims of trafficking in persons,[h]	Eligible.	Same as food stamps/SNAP.	Eligible for 5 years after entry. Eligible at state option after 5 years.	Eligible for 7 years after entry. Eligible at state option after 7 years.
—aliens in temporary protected status, in extended voluntary departure (EVD) status, or deferred enforced departure (DED) status.	Ineligible.	Ineligible, unless in receipt of SSI benefits August 22, 1996.	Ineligible.	Eligible only for emergency services.

Class of Alien	Food Stamps/SNAP	SSI	TANF	Medicaid
Nonimmigrants[i]	Ineligible.	Ineligible.	Ineligible.	Eligible only for emergency services.
Unauthorized aliens[j]	Ineligible.	Ineligible.	Ineligible.	Eligible only for emergency services.
Naturalized aliens	Eligible on naturalization.	Eligible on naturalization.	Eligible on naturalization.	Eligible on naturalization.

a. A substantial work history consists of 40 "qualifying quarters" of work (credits) calculated as they would be for Social Security eligibility purposes—including work not covered by Social Security and work credited from parents and spouses, but not including work performed after 1996 while receiving federal means-tested benefits like TANF, food stamps/SNAP, or Medicaid. A qualifying quarter is a three-month period of full or part-time work with sufficient income to qualify the earner for credit toward eligibility for Social Security benefits. The qualifying quarter income amount is increased annually, and, for 2001, stands at $830; no more than 4 credit quarters can be earned in any 1 year. The qualifying quarter test takes into account work by an alien's parent before the alien became 18 (including work before the alien was born/adopted) and by the alien's spouse (provided the alien remains married to the spouse or the spouse is deceased).

b. Eligible military personnel, veterans, and immediate family members also must be a legal permanent resident, or an asylee, refugee, Cuban/Haitian entrant, alien whose deportation/removal is being withheld, parolee, or conditional entrant.

c. Includes Amerasians admitted as immigrants who were born in Vietnam during the Vietnam era and fathered by a U.S. citizen—as well as their spouses, children, and certain other immediate family members.

d. Noncitizen "cross-border" American Indians (from Canada or Mexico) are noncitizens who belong to a federally recognized tribe or who were born in Canada and have the right to cross the Canadian-U.S. border unhindered (so-called "Jay Treaty" Indians).

e. Members of a Hmong or Highland Laotian tribe when the tribe assisted U.S. personnel by taking part in military/rescue missions during the Vietnam era—including spouses and unmarried dependent children.

f. Eligible parolees must be paroled for at least 1 year.

g. Eligibility in abuse cases is limited to aliens who have been abused (subject to battery or extreme cruelty) in the U.S. by a spouse or other family/ household member, aliens whose children have been abused, and alien children whose parent has been abused—where the alien has been approved for, or has pending an application/petition with a prima facie case for, immigration preference as a spouse or child or cancellation of removal. The alien cannot be residing with the individual responsible for the abuse, and the agency providing benefits must determine that there is a substantial connection between the abuse and the need for benefits.

h. Eligible for treatment as refugees under the provisions of Section 107 of the Victims of Trafficking and Violence Protection Act of 2000 (P.L. 106-386). Eligible victims of trafficking in persons are those subjected to (1) sex trafficking where the act is induced by force, fraud, or coercion, or the person induced to perform the act is under age 18, or (2) involuntary servitude. If age 18 or older, they must be "certified" as willing to assist in the investigation and prosecution of the trafficker(s) and have made an application for a nonimmigrant "T" visa (or be in the U.S. to ensure the effective prosecution of the trafficker(s)).

i. Nonimmigrants are those admitted temporarily for a limited purpose (e.g., students, visitors, or temporary workers).

j. Unauthorized ("illegal") aliens are those in the U.S. in violation of immigration law for whom no legal relief or recognition has been extended.

Appendix B. Estimated Benefit Usage, by Citizenship, for Selected Years

	Native				Naturalized				Noncitizens			
	1995	1998	2001	2007	1995	1998	2001	2007	1995	1998	2001	2007
Estimated number of recipients (in millions)												
AFDC/TANF	4.25	2.51	1.74	1.41	0.11	0.11	0.08	0.06	0.58	0.35	0.26	0.18
SSI	4.15	4.20	4.33	4.37	0.19	0.32	0.41	0.39	0.47	0.38	0.26	0.28
Medicaid	28.53	25.06	28.30	35.20	0.55	0.79	1.09	1.61	2.54	1.80	1.99	2.74
Food stamps/SNAP	25.11	21.85	16.01	20.50	0.44	0.44	0.55	0.63	2.48	1.47	1.19	1.70
Total population	239.2	244.6	249.1	261.2	7.9	9.9	12.0	15.1	16.6	16.6	16.6	22.2
Percent of total recipients by citizenship category												
AFDC/TANF	86.0	84.4	83.8	85.6	2.3	3.9	3.7	3.4	11.8	11.8	12.4	11.1
SSI	86.2	85.8	86.6	86.7	3.9	6.5	8.1	7.8	9.9	7.8	5.3	5.6
Medicaid	90.2	90.6	90.2	89.0	1.7	2.8	3.5	4.1	8.0	6.5	6.3	6.9
Food stamps/SNAP	89.6	90.6	90.2	89.8	1.6	2.2	3.1	2.8	8.9	7.2	6.7	7.5
Percent of receipt within citizenship category												
AFDC/TANF	2.3	1.3	0.9	0.5	1.5	1.2	0.7	0.4	3.9	2.3	1.4	0.8
SSI	2.3	2.3	2.3	1.7	2.4	3.3	3.5	2.6	3.2	2.5	1.4	1.3
Medicaid	11.9	10.2	11.4	13.4	6.9	8.0	9.1	10.7	15.3	10.9	9.7	12.3
Food stamps/SNAP	10.5	7.6	6.4	7.8	5.6	4.5	4.6	4.2	14.9	8.9	5.8	7.7

Source: CRS analysis of CPS March Supplements, 1996, 1999, 2002, and 2008.

Note: Food stamp data are by households; all other data are individuals. Welfare includes AFDC, TANF and general cash assistance.

Appendix C. "Qualified Aliens"

The 1996 welfare law divided noncitizens into two general categories for purposes of benefit eligibility. The least restrictive category is that of *qualified aliens*, a category that, despite its name, is subject to numerous limitations and does not itself indicate eligibility for assistance. Qualified aliens are legal permanent residents, refugees, aliens paroled into the United States for at least one year, and aliens granted asylum or related relief. The 1996 immigration law added certain abused spouses and children as another class, and P.L. 105-33 added Cuban-Haitian entrants.

The other, more restrictive category is that of *non-qualified aliens*. It consists of other noncitizens, including unauthorized (illegal) aliens, nonimmigrants (i.e., aliens admitted for a temporary purpose, such as education or employment), short-term parolees, asylum applicants, and various classes of aliens granted temporary permission to remain. Non-qualified aliens generally are ineligible for almost all federal assistance provided directly to households or individuals. Limited exceptions include emergency medical services and disaster relief.[47]

In general, qualified aliens compose the "universe" of potentially eligible noncitizens. As noted below and in the earlier portions of this report, however, these aliens must, in most cases, pass another test to gain eligibility. In addition, some classes of noncitizens who are not specifically listed as qualified aliens (e.g., Hmong/Highland Laotians, Vietnam-born Amerasians fathered by U.S. citizens) are indeed eligible for benefits. Qualified aliens are subject to eligibility restrictions that vary by program (see **Appendix A**) and may be subject to sponsor-to-alien deeming rules that affect their financial eligibility for aid (noted earlier in this report).

- To gain eligibility for food stamps/SNAP, qualified aliens must (1) have a substantial work history or military connection; (2) have been resident in the United States as of August 22, 1996, and meet certain age or disability requirements; or (3) be within seven years of entry (e.g., if a refugee/asylee).

- To gain eligibility for SSI, qualified aliens must (1) have a substantial work history or military connection; (2) have been an SSI recipient as of August 22, 1996; (3) have been resident in the United States as of August 22, 1996, and be disabled; or (3) be within seven years of entry (e.g., if a refugee/asylee).

- To gain eligibility for TANF, qualified aliens must (1) have a substantial work history or military connection; (2) be in a state that has chosen to allow eligibility to those resident as of August 22, 1996, and/or new entrants who have been resident five years; or (3) be within five years of entry (e.g., if a refugee/asylee). New entrants are not eligible for five years after entry.

- To gain eligibility for Medicaid, qualified aliens must (1) have a substantial work history or military connection; (2) be in a state that has chosen to allow eligibility to those resident as of August 22, 1996, and/or new entrants who have been resident five years; or (3) be within seven years of entry (e.g., if a refugee or asylee). For Medicaid and CHIP, new entrants are not eligible for 5 years after entry, except in the states that have opted to cover children and pregnant LPRs.

---

[47] For discussion of these legislative activities, see CRS Report RL33102, *Federal Food Assistance in Disasters: Hurricanes Katrina and Rita*, by Joe Richardson.

However, for CHIP, the five-year ban is the only additional citizenship-related eligibility requirement that must be met by qualified aliens.

Author Contact Information

Ruth Ellen Wasem
Specialist in Immigration Policy
rwasem@crs.loc.gov, 7-7342

Acknowledgments

CRS Graphics Specialist Amber Wilhelm prepared the figures.